£6.50

Ben,

A souvenir of your visit!

Best wishes,

Those Were the Days
VOLUME II
more collected images from the Isle *of* Man's past

Published by:

Lily Publications, PO Box 33,
Ramsey, Isle of Man IM99 4LP Tel: +44 (0) 1624 898446
Fax: +44 (0) 1624 898449

E-mail: info@lilypublications.co.uk
Website: www.lilypublications.co.uk

Richard Davis

Introduction

In volume one of 'Those Were The Days', I included a few images from the Keig Collection which had recently been acquired by the publisher, Lily Publications. Since then I have been given access to many hundreds of pictures in the collection, and the balance is now reversed so that most of the pictures in 'Those Were The Days Volume 2' are from the Keig archives.

Keig's photographers was established in 1860 by Thomas Keig (1833-1896), who turned his hobby of photography into a business. He was a well-respected member of the local community and became the first mayor of Douglas in 1896, having previously been a long-standing Town Commissioner.

Over the years Keigs built up an impressive collection of pictures, reflecting many aspects of life on the Isle of Man. That the early scenes are predominantly centred on Douglas is no surprise; many of the public transport facilities we now take for granted were completely absent until the late 1800s, and the first private motor car did not arrive until 1889.

Isle of Man Railways' Douglas to Peel line opened in 1873, with Port Erin following in 1874 and Ramsey, via the Manx Northern Railway, in 1879. The Douglas & Laxey Coast Electric Tramway opened as far as Groudle in 1893, with extensions to Laxey in 1894 and to Ramsey in 1899. Prior to that, the only alternative to walking was by horse-drawn or steam-hauled vehicle, or by boat. A photographer might think twice about loading a cumbersome and heavy camera and tripod, with a stock of fragile 10 x 8 inch glass plate negatives - almost A4 size in modern terms - for a journey by pony and trap, or perhaps by boat, to say Port Erin or Ramsey in order to take some pictures! In any event, there were other photographers at work in the principal towns of the Island.

Many of the images in this volume have been taken from original glass negatives, some dating back more than 150 years.

Most of the negatives have become scratched or have other blemishes due to age, handling, and less than ideal storage conditions, but following high-definition scanning, the worst of the damage has been corrected to recover what would in many cases have been unusable images.

I am greatly indebted to renowned local historians Peter Kelly and Stan Basnett for background information for many of the captions; and to Miles Cowsill at Lily Publications and Charles Guard of the Manx Heritage Foundation for their personal involvement with the book.

Richard Davis
November 2013

DOUGLAS 1868

This view of Douglas, taken from Douglas Head, is dated 1868 and shows work continuing on the construction of the Queen Victoria Pier. Beyond it can be seen the Iron Pier at the bottom of Broadway. It was completed and opened in 1869 with a wooden pavilion on the seaward end. The pier was dismantled in the winter of 1893-4, and different reports claim that it was either re-erected at Rhos-on-Sea, or that it was scrapped by a Manchester scrap metal merchant. The pavilion was re-erected at the entrance to Groudle Glen as Dobie's Cafe. To the left of the picture are the Red Pier and the Fort Anne Jetty (erected in 1837). Harris Promenade had just been constructed while Loch Promenade did not exist at this time, and a series of 'slips' ran down to the beach.

A view of Douglas taken in about 1880 showing the Queen Victoria Pier, opened 1872, and Loch Promenade, which dates from 1878. The Iron Pier, at the bottom of Broadway, built 1869, is also visible. An interesting feature of this image is that someone has used a bit of artistic licence on the original glass negative, adding the Falcon Cliff Pavilion which was not built until shortly after the photograph was taken, only to be demolished in 1896. (The pavilion can be seen just to the left of the Falcon Cliff Hotel, towards the right side of the picture).

Douglas in 1878. In this view, some of the numerous public houses in North Quay can be identified, amongst them the Black Lion Hotel, the Greyhound Hotel and the Cheshire Inn. Old St Matthew's Church and the Market Place are towards the right centre, with St Barnabas far right. On the skyline are the spires of (left to right) The Bethel (Circular Road), St Mary's (Bucks Road), and St Andrew's (Finch Road). Bucks Road Primitive Methodist Church and Rosemount Wesleyan Church are yet to be built. St Thomas' Church and Loch Parade Church can be made out on the right-hand side of the picture.

A busy scene on North Quay, Douglas, with coal being unloaded from a sailing ship onto a horse-drawn cart. The cart is inscribed: 'W. K. Kermode, Bridge Coal Yard No.3, Douglas'. Mr. Kermode set up his business around 1872 and from his profits bought Eyreton Farm at Crosby. His men were employed on the farm in the summer months when coal wasn't selling, and then on the coal deliveries in the winter. Unlike other photographs of the quay, most of the buildings shown here still exist. Note the upright piece of stone in the lower centre of the picture, used to tie mooring ropes around.

In this view, the swing bridge across Douglas Harbour, built by Armstrong-Mitchell of Newcastle in 1895, is having the steel deck fitted. The 450 ton, 176 feet long bridge was used both by pedestrians and horse-drawn carriages on payment of a toll, and was often referred to as the 'halfpenny bridge'.

WOODHOUSE TERRACE SOUTH QUAY 1920

Although dated 1920, this view of Woodhouse Terrace fits in well with the other images as it gives a good idea of how the South Quay looked around the turn of the 19th-20th century. The swing bridge is out of view to the left of the picture. It was here that Moses Hampton sold oil and petrol in cans. Later all these properties were demolished to become the site of the Esso depot. It is currently a cleared site awaiting redevelopment. On the skyline are houses in Taubman Terrace on the way up to Douglas Head.

THE OLD MARKET PLACE DOUGLAS

Lots of activity in this scene on the North Quay with market stalls, St Matthew's Church (centre) and the Douglas Hotel to the right. This was originally built for a Mr. Black, a rich Scottish merchant, in the days before the Revestment Act. It was later bought by the Duke of Atholl before he built the Castle Mona. James Street, with the Artisan's Dwellings built by the Town Commissioners, is to the left, with Market Hill running left-to-right beside the church. On the extreme left is a French-style circular cast iron gentlemen's urinal.

St Mathew's old church Douglas

Douglas Market Place with old St Matthew's Church and Chapel Row behind - Market Hill is on the extreme left. The Market Hotel can be seen to the right of the church. The church was built in 1708 and demolished in 1897 to make way for the cast iron butter and fish market built in 1900. On the gable of the church, set into the wall, was a drinking fountain which bore the inscription '1860 St Matthew's Drinking Fountain'. This was recycled and built into the corner of the brick-built butchers' market of 1899, where it still survives.

THE BUTTER MARKET

Another view of the Market Place with Chapel Row to the right and Market Hill centre. The shadow of St Matthew's Church can be seen on the wall of the Douglas Medical Hall, which, by the time of the photograph, had become Young's Chemist and Market Place Post Office. It is interesting that the bills posted on the gable of the demolished property are mainly for English products, with few for local shops or places of entertainment.

A familiar Douglas scene, but with a difference. The Jubilee Clock, donated by George Dumbell of Dumbell's Bank and erected in 1887, is in view, and horse trams are running on the promenade, but the cable car tracks in Victoria Street have yet to be laid to transport passengers to upper Douglas. Behind the clock is a horse-drawn omnibus which was one of several that travelled to the Isle of Man International Exhibition at Belle Vue (opened 1892). The cable cars appeared in 1896.

The Queen Victoria Pier at the height of the Edwardian era, when tourism reached its peak with passenger arrivals on the Island around the half-million mark annually. The ship on the left of the picture is the Midland Railway steamer *Manxman* arriving from Heysham. The other is almost certainly *Douglas* (III) of the IoM Steam Packet Co. In front of it is one of the steam ferries that plied to and from the Battery Pier to take passengers to Douglas Head. The fare was 1d (one old penny).

These two photographs show work in progress on the construction of the Queen Victoria Pier extension, commenced in 1887. The top photograph shows concrete blockmaking in the Harbour Board yard alongside Approach Road, where fifteen-ton blocks were cast and then loaded onto a barge to be taken across the harbour to the works. Note the vertical-boiler steam crane on the harbourside for lowering the blocks.

The lower photograph, taken in 1894 as the pier was nearing completion, shows the 'Hercules' steam crane at work placing a block in position. When this was finished the crane was shipped to Peel to build the breakwater there.

Victoria Pier Arcade fully opened by 1893, with the glass canopy added in 1908. It was demolished and replaced in winter phases by the Sea Terminal building, completed in 1965. Some of the bricks from the building were salvaged and cleaned by a local builder who used them in the construction of two bungalows in St. Ninian's Road. The four-faced clock was put in storage and, over twenty years later, returned to the maker! Image from the author's collection.

FALCON CLIFF   FREE ALL DAY

The shore at Harris Promenade, Douglas (formerly Colonel's Road). The Iron Pier, opened in 1869, is not in this view, having been dismantled during the winter of 1893-4, but the Falcon Cliff Ballroom can still be seen on the centre skyline (see inset). When the Palace, Derby Castle and Falcon Cliff and Pavilion companies merged in 1898 the Monstre Pavilion of the Falcon Cliff was taken down and sold in order to concentrate entertainment at promenade level. The lift was also sold and went to Port Soderick where the two cars were used as kiosks adjacent to the hotel, new cars being provided to work on the reassembled lift. A second lift was installed at Falcon Cliff in 1927. On the left of the picture is the bandstand for pierrot performances.

Above: This view is a little further along the promenade, and is taken from the elevated Iron Pier. Donkey rides, pop stall and bathing huts are available. Beside the billboard is a drinking fountain and then a cast iron gentlemen's urinal. Built as private residences in the 1840s, the terraces of houses are by now used to take in visitors. The Castle Mona and Falcon Cliff Hotels can be seen in the background. Central Promenade was opened in 1896.

Right: At the bottom of Broadway the original twin lodges to the Duke of Atholl's Castle Mona have taken on a commercial role as the Castle Tap public house and Bennett's American Bowling Saloon. The original drive passed between them and became Castle Mona Avenue. Shortly after this photograph was taken all the properties to the left were demolished, and Louis Kelly built the Central Hotel which was opened in July 1888.

THE CASTLE TAP BROADWAY 1887

Left: Thomas Unsworth's fruit, vegetable and confectioner's shop on Broadway lay within H. B. Noble's Villa Marina grounds. In the space behind the shop was the kitchen garden of the house, as shown in the next photograph.

Below: A 1910 view of the Villa Marina, taken from Broadway. The house was originally a private dwelling called Marina Lodge. Later, it was used as a school and then for a short time as the Governor's residence. Latterly owned by Douglas philanthropist Henry Bloom Noble, the estate passed to Douglas Corporation in 1910, and the house was demolished to make way for the great public hall named the Villa Marina (see next picture).

The Villa Marina Kursaal was opened on 19th July 1913, but some work appears to be still ongoing in this view, despite the signs outside advertising the grand opening. The contractor's board (Paul Rhodes, Leeds) is still visible on the extreme right. Paul Rhodes and Sons went on to build houses in Allan Street, Circular Road, Westmoreland Road and Princes Street for Douglas Corporation, and the Douglas High School for Boys at St. Ninians. The Germanic name *Kursaal* was quietly dropped at the outbreak of World War One the following year. Note that the main entrance to the complex was by way of external steps on the front of the building. Many years later the building received a new glass front entrance with internal staircases.

OPENING OF VILLA MARINA DOUGLAS

Above: The Harris Promenade entrance to the Villa Marina in 1913. At this stage the colonnade and arcade had yet to be built; these followed in 1931. The two pay kiosks with turnstiles and central gates matched the two on Broadway which still exist to this day.

Left: The opening of the Villa Marina, 19th July 1913. In this view Lady Raglan, the Governor's wife, has just turned on the marble fountain, placed there to commemorate the visit to Douglas in 1902 by King Edward VII and Queen Alexandra. Made out of white marble with a Celtic design on the side, it was carved by Roystons of Peel Road, and in the 1930s was repositioned in the gardens by the Broadway entrance where it still remains.

ENTRANCE TO FALCON CLIFF AND THE PALLACE

A photograph that captures the development of Douglas as a holiday destination. Built in the grounds of the Castle Mona Hotel is the 'Palace', which opened in 1889. On the right is the promenade entrance to the Falcon Cliff Hotel; the adjoining Monstre Pavilion opened in August 1883. The following year a two-car lift was constructed to take patrons up to the entertainment via the entrance shown. The man facing the camera stands on McCrone's slip at the start of the Queen's Promenade widening, which was officially opened in July 1890. Billboards for the Falcon Cliff show Lester Barrett, a popular music hall performer and Mlle Vonare the 'marvellous lady contortionist', who appeared together in June 1891. Directly behind the man is a wall, with balustrade above, where the Castle Mona shops were built in 1898.

THE PALACE BEFORE THE SHOPS WERE MADE

This view of Central Promenade shows the Palace Ballroom prior to the building of shops on the promenade frontage. The Castle Mona Hotel can be seen in the centre of the picture. The raised grass bank was originally a gun emplacement, used in conjunction with gun batteries on Douglas Head and on Onchan Head, where the Royal Skandia building stands today. The embankment was partly removed when the Palace Shops were built, and when the Palace Hotel was later built on the site in the mid-1960s several of the cannons were unearthed.

LITTLE SWITZERLAND DOUGLAS

In this photograph, taken about 1906, the appropriately-named Edelweiss boarding house sits at the bottom of Switzerland Road where it meets Queen's Promenade. Within the hotel is Clague's grocery shop, which in the 1960s was run by the hotel owners as Anna's Tea Room. Beside it are the premises of Metropole Garage Motor Tours, which were swept away in 1911 when shops with flats above were built. On the right is Mona Cottage, which was extended until it became a 38-bedroom licensed guest house. From 1908 onwards the owner, a Mr Tyson, applied to Douglas Corporation for permission to build five shops around and in front of his property at promenade level. He was finally given permission in May 1910. The greater part of the extension was the Swiss Cafe, which also had a terraced area on the flat roof. Today it is a tee-shirt shop, and Mona Cottage still stands.

A view of Derby Castle (right) and what became King Edward Road, under construction in 1892. The large double building in the roadway at the bottom of Summer Hill is the original horse tram terminus and tram-sheds. Port-e-Vada creek has been blocked from the sea by the road construction. Once it had been filled in, the depot and power station for the Douglas and Laxey Electric Coast Tramway, opened in 1893, was built on the site. On the right of the photograph a wall is being constructed around the low level ground which became the basement under the Theatre of Varieties, built as an extension of the Derby Castle. On the left is an iron pier which was used, not for landing boats, but as a safe platform for the firework displays at Derby Castle. The whole Derby Castle complex was demolished in the late 1960s to make way for the Aquadrome and Summerland.

An 1893 view of Derby Castle, the new promenade and King Edward Road with the Iron Pier (right), which was carried away by a storm later that year. On the headland to the right the Douglas Bay Hotel (now the site of Royal Skandia) is yet to be built, and Imperial Terrace (now the site of a large block of apartments) is also yet to be started.

In the area bounded by present-day Parade Street, North Quay, Fort Street and Ridgeway Street there was a sprawling network of little streets, public houses and courtyards, nearly all of which had become slums. In 1922 the Island's Government passed the Douglas Town Improvement Act, giving the Corporation powers to clear the area and build a new access road into the town. Demolition did not start until 1929 because the Act required that displaced residents should be re-housed. This was achieved by building at Pulrose, Olympia and the Hills Estate. There seems to have been a concerted effort to record some of the scenes, as there are several batches of photographs taken in this area in the Keig Collection.

This is one of a series of photographs taken by Thomas Keig at the time of the six-acre demolition of Georgian Douglas, showing Fancy Street in 1895. In modern day terms it is the lane running behind the properties opposite the Town Hall. In fact a street named to that effect is now in place. It linked Lord Street and King Street, and this view is towards the Imperial Vaults in Lord Street. On the left is the former wine and spirit store of James Gell, the licensed grocer of nearby Victoria Street.

Although Thomas Keig wrote 'Post Office Place 1896' on this photograph, taken just before the old Post Office and adjoining properties were demolished, it was in fact officially Post Office Lane. It ran diagonally from Lord Street down to James Street, and this building was located at what is now the end of Coronation Terrace. The Post Office was run by the Graves family from 1805.

QUINES CORNER 1912

Quine's Corner in 1912, with what had been Sam Quine's pub in the centre of the picture. To the right, Big Well Street leads up towards the Athol Street junction. Coming up to Quine's Corner is Queen Street, with the roof of Corlett Sons and Cowley's large warehouse showing at the top of the picture. Big Well Street continued to the left until it met with the junction of Barrack Street and Hanover Street.

ST BARNABAS SQUARE DOUGLAS 1912

This photograph was taken by T. S. Keig in 1912, looking into St Barnabas Square from the bottom of Duke Lane (later absorbed into Lord Street). The side of the original Town Hall can be seen, with Fort Street beyond. Behind the wall on the right were several houses owned by the Spittall family; it was in one of these that H. B. Noble lived when he first came to the Island.

LEWTHWAITES COURT FORT STREET DOUGLAS 1912

Lewthwaite's Court, off Fort Street, in 1912. Whoever lived there must have been a porter, judging by the luggage cart. These carts often feature in Keig images taken in this part of Douglas, as it was near to the piers. Such carts were in use until the late 1960s-early 70s, and would be piled high with visitors' luggage. The porter would push the cart the length of Douglas Promenade to deliver the bags and cases, while the visitors travelled to their hotel by horse tram.

Fort Street in 1912, so named as it led to the fort (demolished 1818) on Pollock Rock which offered protection to the harbour. One of the oldest streets in the town, it was originally bounded by the sea on the right of this view until Loch Promenade was built. The property on the left is part of the Sheffield Hotel which faced onto Parade Street. On the right is the property of Mr. J. McMullin, who would operated horse-drawn vehicles and subsequently motor charabancs for another fifty years.

DRURY LANE DOUGLAS 1912

A 1912 view of Drury Lane, which ran from the North Quay towards New Bond Street. Many of the old streets of Douglas twisted and turned which, although not easy for horse-drawn vehicles, did cut down on the wind blowing through the streets. The two ladies stand in front of an advertisement for Zebrite Grate Blacking. All the buildings seen in this photograph were demolished in the 1930s and lie beneath what we still call the bus station area.

BOND LANE DOUGLAS 1912

In this 1912 view Bond Lane leads out of the centre of the photograph and is viewed from Drury Lane. North Quay is behind the photographer. Note the number of small shops that were to be found in most of these streets, and also yet another porter's cart. The former Hare and Hounds Inn is the building set back in the right foreground. All this area, which included numerous public houses, was cleared in the 1930s.

NORTH QUAY DOUGLAS 1912

The Double Corner on North Quay in 1912, featuring several properties demolished in the mid-1930s. Many of these buildings were public houses, such as the Oddfellows' Arms and the Liverpool and Manchester Arms. To the left of them, the Billiard Saloon was the original office of the Isle of Man Steam Packet Company. The opening behind the lamp-post (centre) is Drury Lane.

Right: New Bond Street took its name from the nearby bonded warehouse located under the Douglas Hotel, which was the Customs House. On the right is the Step Down Inn, whilst the building opposite, with the porch, was the Douglas Grammar School. It was here that the father of T. E. Brown, the Manx National Poet, taught whilst chaplain of nearby St. Matthew's Church.

Below: One of the oldest streets in Douglas, Muckles Gate still survives as the lane behind the Manx Co-op in Duke Street and then becomes Cambrian Place at the sharp left-and-right turn. At the end of Muckles Gate are the Widows' Cottages which, after the demolition of the properties in the foreground, faced onto the 'yellow bus' station.

Douglas Head Steam Ferries *Thistle*, *Rose* and *Shamrock* laid up in the inner harbour, with Lake Road on the left, Bank's Circus and the railway station to the right. The two houses on the left of the terrace in between were demolished by Douglas Corporation in the 1950s and replaced by flats with a mansard roof. The building on the right of the terrace is the Railway Hotel, built by Charles Udall, the developer of the Villiers Hotel on Loch Promenade a couple of years later. Note the structure on the wall in front which incorporates a drinking fountain and cast iron gentlemen's urinal facing onto Bridge Road. Clinch's Brewery is on the extreme right.

North Quay, near its junction with Ridgeway Street, showing work on the harbour wall. The two men were obviously connected with the project as they appear on other images in the Keig Collection. Note the huge blocks of stone that have been lifted out of the quayside wall by the crane and stacked on the road. In the background, behind the crane, St Matthew's Church Hall of 1912 is yet to be built.

Elsewhere in the town major works were in hand to lay a new trunk sewer. This is Marina Road (now part of Castle Street) looking towards Broadway with the gable of the promenade shelter just visible (centre right) behind the spoil heaps. Note how not every property in the street was commercial; on the extreme left, there are railings to the front garden of a house on the corner of St Thomas' Walk. On the other side of this is the building which is now Sam Webb's public house.

Ridgeway Street in 1912, with the Prospect Hill/ Victoria Street junction in the background. The recently-built Town Hall is to the left, with Lowey's grocers at the entrance to John Street beneath the 'Examiner' printing works. The shop in the centre background is R. D. Cowin's bakers. The protruding lamp on the front of the Ridgeway Hotel, built in 1895, can just be seen on the extreme right. On the skyline to the right of the St Andrew's spire is Thomas Keig's astronomical observatory on the roof of his Prospect Hill property.

This well-known photograph shows the bottom of Prospect Hill, with an Upper Douglas cable car just beginning the ascent. Opened in 1896, the system closed in 1929. The building on the left was Dumbell's Bank, which opened in 1861 as Dumbell and Howard's Douglas and Isle of Man Bank. As Dumbell's Bank it crashed in 1900, with far-reaching consequences for many Manx families and businesses. In the centre of the picture is Belfast House, a five storey boarding house set above James Kissack's grocery store. It was built in 1888 to the designs of the Liverpool architect John Clarke. The upper floors were partly rebuilt in the late 1970s, when the tower was removed.

PROSPECT HILL 1895

This 1895 view was taken a little further up Prospect Hill, and prior to the laying of the cable car track. Kissack's shop, on the left of the picture, features a promotion on 'Fine Old Scotch Whisky' which is on offer at 3/- (three shillings or today 15p) per bottle. It was in one of the three shops above this that Thomas Keig had his first photographic shop and studio, first with his partner, a Mr. Collister, and then by himself. Note that in this view Belfast House is captioned 'Argyle Boarding House', though it was referred to as Belfast House in a 1903 licensing application.

Moving further up Prospect Hill we come to the Athol Street/Prospect Hill junction in this 1893 view. The spire of St Andrew's Church is in the right background. The Isle of Man Bank, opened in 1902, still occupies the corner site today. In this view the Athol Street Post Office is on the end of the block, with Cain, bookseller, and Clarke, saddler nearby. The tall block with the decorative frontage was built by a Mr. Fell on some of the first plots in Athol Street to be developed. The section on the right was originally gardens; it was demolished to make way for the cable car tracks and the whole property was boarded up and plastered with posters.

Athol Street from a slightly different angle, taken from a badly-damaged magic lantern slide in the author's collection. Premises featured are, left to right: James Hales, tailors and drapers (6 Athol Street), Miss Cubbon, dyers (4 Athol Street), Charles Wallace, watchmaker (2 Athol Street), and Joseph Clarke, saddler. In a photograph obviously taken before the days of Health and Safety, the two painters stand on a single plank set between two stepladders (lettered W. Gell Painter - also of Athol Street) to work on the sign board of Clarke's premises.

Continuing our journey up Prospect Hill, we look downhill towards the Athol Street corner which is just visible on the extreme left. The side elevation of William Fell's building is on the end of Athol Street - all these windows did indeed have a great 'prospect' over Douglas Bay from their location on Prospect Hill. The single-storey shops were built in the original garden to the property. On the right is the premises of Austin Bucknall who, prior to his shop being demolished to make way for the cable car tracks, built a large warehouse in Athol Street, taken over some years later by Manningtons. His son Joseph set up business in Upper Church Street and the firm continues to this day. Photo courtesy of Morrisons Photographers (but also a Keig photo).

At the junction of Circular Road and Bucks Road we see the Raglan Hotel, which started life as a boarding house like its neighbours except that the front door was on the side facing Circular Road rather than on Bucks Road. It had three sitting rooms and ten bedrooms in 1887 when the proprietor Mr F. P. Johns applied for a public house licence. He stated at the time that he intended to add a further six bedrooms, a bar and a parlour. These show on the photograph with the three arched openings to the right of the down-pipe facing Circular Road. Coming up the hill is a rare sight of cable car No. 82, one of the closed winter cars introduced in 1896. The Raglan and its neighbour were demolished and replaced by the Standard Bank.

CABLE TRAM

Another view of an Upper Douglas cable car, this time of the open variety. The location is Woodbourne Road, with Salisbury Terrace on the left. York Road junction at Avondale Corner is visible in the mid-background with Ballaquayle Road in the far distance. Newsham Terrace (beyond York Road, on the left) has yet to be built in this view. The cable tramway turned down York Road to its depot and on into Broadway. The large house on the skyline was called Belle Vue, and was demolished in 1911 to become part of the site of St Ninian's Church which was opened in 1913. Opposite the end of Woodbourne Road is the original lodge to Laureston House.

The Old Records Office in St Barnabas Square, built in 1820, became Douglas Town Commissioners' Office in 1860 and then had an extra floor added to provide a meeting room for the commissioners. Years later it became the Customs House. St Barnabas' Church, which can be seen in the background, was built in 1832 and demolished in 1969.

In this view taken in John Street outside the then new Town Hall, Douglas Fire Brigade assembles with the horse-drawn manual fire engine 'DOUGLAS' for the coronation celebrations of King Edward VII in August 1902. Beneath the banner displaying a crown can be seen the front door to the Town Hall, which in the 1920s was moved to its present position in Ridgeway Street. The horses used to pull the fire engine were kept in the Corporation Yard behind the Villiers Hotel, and when they were called out had to be harnessed and brought up to John Street before the brigade could set off to the fire.

The Devil's Elbow in Strand Street was at its junction with Drumgold Street. This photograph was taken in 1886 in Strand Street, looking towards the Duke Street junction. The projecting properties were the subject of many letters to the local press with calls for the Town Commissioners to force the owner to pull down the properties and set them back. In the end the commissioners spent £4000 buying the various properties and a further £600 on demolition and setting back. The cleared plot was sold to Louis Kelly the builder for redevelopment, for £2560, in March 1887. The building at No. 3, Kelly's boot and shoe maker, was demolished soon after this picture was taken.

ARCH LANE (GUTTERY GABLE)

Arch Lane, also known as Guttery Gable, was located in Strand Street. This view predates the erection of the Strand Cinema (opened 1913) and is taken from Howard Street, with Strand Street running across the picture. The lane provided a convenient access to Market Street. The nearby Picture House, opened in 1921, had an overhead enclosed gangway spanning Guttery Gable and connecting to the Strand Cinema. During recent development of the site the facade of the cinema was retained and the lane was repositioned to the right of the building - still bearing the name Guttery Gable.

Above: Quine's Corner takes its name from Samuel Quine, who owned land at the top end of North Quay in the 1790s. These photographs were taken in 1929, when properties were being demolished wholesale in Big Well Street and Hanover Street to make way for the very wide road Lord Street. This would become a principal route into Douglas via the equally wide Peel Road. Running across the background are properties in Shaw's Brow, which in turn stand behind the houses and offices in Athol Street. Following the clearance large blocks of flats were erected for Douglas Corporation by the Universal Housing Company. The architect was Jos. E. Teare, who had as pupils Wilfred Quayle, Tom Kennaugh and Frank O'Hanlon, all of whom went on to leave their mark on the Island.

Right: A closer view of Quine's Corner in 1930, with some slight changes to the previous image. The corner shop is now boarded up prior to demolition. The new shops and flats which took its place were completed by 1932.

BIG WELL STREET 1929

Big Well Street, Douglas, following demolition in 1929. Douglas Railway Station can be seen in the distance, and Quine's Corner on the left, but little else remained of the 34 properties in the street after this area was cleared as part of the Lord Street redevelopment. The land to the right is now partly occupied by the Lord Street flats and partly by Shaw's Brow car park.

Peveril Buildings, built in 1889 on the site of Twemlow's Yard. Clyde House, on the right, later became the Warwick Hotel, and the three shops on the ground floor are now part of a night club. To the left is the side of the Peveril Hotel, which was extended along the Loch Promenade elevation and taken up an extra floor in 1887. Note the ever-popular oyster bar on the ground floor. The end section appears to be run as a separate boarding house called Bousfield House.

Left: The Douglas Head terminus of the Douglas Southern Electric Tramway (later Douglas Head Marine Drive), which opened in 1896 and closed in September 1939. Power car No. 1, now resident at Crich Tramway Village in Derbyshire, is the only survivor of the eight double-decker power cars and trailers on the line.

Below: The Battery Pier (completed 1879) in the background gives a clue to the site of this amusement arcade, which was at the bottom of the steps leading to Douglas Head from Approach Road. The Incline Railway lower terminus was to the right of the picture. To the left of the picture was the battery of cannons which protected the harbour; hence the name of the pier.

Here we see construction work at the 'new' Douglas Bridge, completed in 1937. In this view, the arch of the old stone bridge of 1778 can still be seen in the centre, while South Quay is the name of the terrace of houses running across the back of the picture. Built between the 1790s and around 1810, these were the most fashionable houses in the town at the time. On the right is the corrugated iron building used by Qualtrough and Co. as their mineral water (pop) works. Previously it had been a boat-building works. Notice the baby in the pram parked on the extreme left as Mum looks at the work going on below.

The Athol Hotel on the corner of Regent Street viewed from the sea side of Loch Promenade. After widening by 100 feet (30metres), the new promenade was opened on 23 June, 1934. The former Empire Theatre, which closed in 1929, can be seen halfway down Regent Street. The Athol and its neighbours were demolished at the same time as the Villiers Hotel and at the moment this remains a vacant site. Panelling and stained glass from the smoke room bar of the Athol are now in 'The Cat With No Tail' pub at Governor's Hill.

HILLS HOUSE CIRCULAR ROAD DOUGLAS 1923

Hills House on Circular Road, Douglas, at the junction with Westmoreland Road, pictured in 1923, the year before it was demolished. It was once the home of the wealthy Moore family, and for many years was regarded as being outside the town of Douglas. St George's Church was built on one of the fields belonging to the house. The name Hills is perpetuated in the name of one of the Wards of Douglas for polling purposes. The site of all these properties is now occupied by Douglas Corporation housing, which extends round the corner into Westmoreland Road.

HILLS GARDENS DOUGLAS

This view over the Hills Estate shows the new Noble's Hospital, opened in September 1912. The whole of the area was used as allotments, as were other parts of the town. Only the Ballakermeen allotments behind St. Catherine's Drive survive today. Hillside Avenue and adjacent streets were built to accommodate some of those displaced by the clearances in lower Douglas. The bellcote of the Mission Hall in Allan Street is in the right background. This was run by St George's Church and like the Barrack Street Mission Hall (now 'The Outback') was used for prayer meetings and social gatherings. It was not required after the building of All Saints Church (the Tin Tab) higher up in the town, and became the Rechabite Hall. It is now an architect's office.

An interesting view of the end of Athol Street showing No. 70 (the end house), home of world-famous artist and Art Nouveau designer Archibald Knox. He died in 1933 and the house was subsequently demolished (see next picture), together with the adjoining house in Peel Road. The road was widened and a garden created on the remaining land. In 1983, 50 years after the death of Archibald Knox, the Isle of Man Victorian Society erected a commemorative plaque on the gable of 68, shown here as the Station Cafe.

Demolition work in progress on 70 Athol Street, Douglas, which in those days was very much a slow job undertaken by hand. The adjoining house in Peel Road has already gone, revealing Athol Terrace. In the lane behind Knox's house were several cottages running the length of St George's Walk. The trees in the left side of the picture were in the garden of 'The Hermitage', later to become 'Cunningham House', headquarters of the Isle of Man Boy Scouts and Girl Guides' Association.

RESULT OF COLLAPSE OF WALL BIG WELL STREET

On Big Well Street. The corner of Athol Street is just visible on the extreme left, and the back of No. 57A, a red brick building shown on the right. In the mid-1960s this became part of the Isle of Man Bank Trustee Department, and later the temporary bank of Julian S. Hodge. In the foreground is the Station Post Office, of which the last sub-postmaster before its demolition was a Mr. Corlett. The site of this collection of buildings is now a garden with a water feature at the junction of Athol Street and Lord Street.

Belle Vue Racecourse, which later became King George V Park, had an imposing entrance on Pulrose Road. The sign on the left was probably 'Race Course', referring to the horse-racing which took place there from 1912 until 1931. The site had previously been the Belle Vue International Exhibition which, in addition to exhibition halls, had a circus and a replica of Lord Nelson's HMS *Victory* which had been brought from an exhibition in London. The Belle Vue venture eventually went bankrupt, and the *Victory* went up in flames in a fire believed to have been started by children. One of the buildings from the exhibition was re-erected at Lower Sulby Farm in Onchan and used as a shed for traction engines. Pulrose Power Station is out of view to the left of this picture.

A view, probably taken around 1950, which shows taxis lined up on the base of King Edward VIII pier waiting for the arrival of the 3pm boat from Liverpool. On the quayside other cars and a coach are parked at a lower level. The arcade building with the clock tower sits at the base of the Victoria Pier which is linked to the Edward Pier by 'The Viaduct', set on legs above Circus Beach. The Pier Arcade was replaced by the Sea Terminal, and the whole area between the piers as shown in this picture has been filled in to become a marshalling yard for vehicles awaiting shipment.

No album of old photographs of the Isle of Man would be complete without some pictures of the Isle of Man Steam Packet Company's vessels.

The *Mona's Isle* ran aground at Scarlett in September 1892, and is seen here being assisted off the rocks at high tide by the *Tynwald*. The ladder between the bow of the ship and the rocks seems rather precarious.

This is one of four close-up pictures of the famously ill-fated *Ellan Vannin*, which sank in a violent storm at the entrance to the River Mersey on 3rd December 1909 with the loss of all on board. As the wreck was in shallow water and presented a hazard to shipping, the vessel was subsequently destroyed by explosives. She was the forerunner of the modern-day Steam Packet in that she carried both passengers and cargo; contemporary ships usually carried either one or the other.

Between the wars the Steam Packet embarked on a series of new-builds which included the *Ben-my-Chree* of 1927 - one of three pre-war ships painted in white livery. She remained in service until 1965. Note the semi-open style of bridge.

The *Mona's Queen*, built in 1934, was one of the Steam Packet ships lost during the evacuation of Dunkirk in May 1940. The first picture shows her as new, while the two smaller pictures below show her just after detonating a mine on the 29th May. The starboard anchor of the ship was raised in 2010 and returned to the Isle of Man as a memorial to the Steam Packet personnel who had lost their lives at Dunkirk. It has been set up at Callow Point, Port St Mary. Note the differing lines in the area of the foredeck, where the other vessels have a distinctive cut-away just ahead of the superstructure.

Above: The *Fenella*, built in 1936, was another casualty, along with the *King Orry*; both were bombed and sunk at Dunkirk in May 1940.

Below: The *Tynwald*, also built in 1936, was another Steam Packet vessel involved in the evacuation of troops at Dunkirk. She had the distinction of evacuating almost 9000 troops, more than any other Steam Packet vessel. She survived this operation and was acquired by the Admiralty, becoming HMS *Tynwald*, only to be sunk by a torpedo from an Italian submarine off the coast of North Africa in November 1941.

S.S. Lady of Manne.

The *Lady of Mann,* seen here in her original white livery, was frequently referred to as the 'Centenary Ship' as she was built in 1930, 100 years after the Steam Packet commenced operations. Returned to the Steam Packet after the war, she remained in service until 1971.

Still on a wartime theme, Palace Terrace was one of several locations requisitioned for the internment of enemy aliens during World War Two. This was part of the Palace Camp; others were at the Sefton, Metropole, Hutchinson Square and Onchan. The wooden posts supporting the barbed wire were set in the asphalt between the tram lines and patched following their removal after the war. This can still be clearly seen at intervals along the promenade to this day. *(Photo courtesy of Morrisons Photographers)*

Following the clearance of six-and-a-half acres of Georgian Douglas in the early 1890s, the Town Commissioners laid out a grid plan of new streets bounded by North Quay, Market Hill, Duke Street, King Street and Ridgeway Street back to North Quay. Lord Street and James Street ran parallel with the quayside. At the junction of Market Hill and Lord Street is one of the brick-built properties in the redevelopment. It was built for J. Cubbon and Son, who had been saddlers but became portmanteau and bag makers. Next door was Lewthwaite's the bookbinders and stationers, who eventually extended into Cubbon's shop and eventually became Manx Stationers.

Boots Cash Chemist opened their first shop in Douglas at 22 Duke Street in 1899. Gradually they moved around the corner into the prime corner site on Victoria Street and then worked their way up the street. They took in Mr. J. Hollis's shoe shop, which he had occupied since 1938. Previously the family had shops in Prospect Terrace, Ridgeway Street, the Villa Marina Arcade, Port St Mary and higher up Victoria Street. Mr. Christen Larsen opened his Cash Outfitters at 39 Victoria Street in 1922. The family had come from Denmark and gradually the business changed to become a high class tailors. Gelling's Foundry moved into Mr. Doyle's Victoria Bazaar on the right of the picture around 1920. At second floor level the shop had a special recess which accommodated a statue of Queen Victoria. This is partly visible at the extreme right edge of the picture, while the canopy of the Regal Cinema can just be seen jutting out over the pavement at the extreme left.

A picture taken at the same time shows a Douglas Corporation bus on route 10 to Upper Douglas at the stop outside Gelling's Foundry, where the group of children sheltering in the doorway in the previous photo has been picked up. Boots closed in 1967 and moved to much smaller temporary premises in Strand Street pending the demolition and rebuilding of these premises. They finally decided to pull out when the Borough Surveyor insisted that the new shop had car parking on the roof. After some years' absence they moved back into their present premises in Strand Street. This group of Victorian buildings remains today.

These were the last shops to be built in Victoria Street. T. H. Colebourn's radio shop was one of three built in the street for a Mr. Colebourn, a cork-cutter and fancy goods dealer. This particular shop, at the junction of Victoria Street and Ridgeway Street, was occupied by Hollis's shoe shop from 1932 to 1938. On the left is Victoria Stores, a grocery business that lasted until the early 1970s. Next door is the Unemployment Registration and Employment Exchange (later Elder's bakers shop) then a children's outfitters. In T. H. Colebourn's window electric kettles are priced at 4/6d (22 ½p) and there isn't a television to be seen! T. H. Colebourn first set up business with a Mr. Kermode in 1923, selling motorcycle parts. The following year they went into wireless sets and moved from Ridgeway Street to 5 Castle Street. When 'T. H.' went by himself in 1934 he was back in Ridgeway Street. His advertisements often carried a portrait of himself, as in the cartoon above the door in this picture.

On 11th April 1951 the Strand Street branch of Woolworths caught fire, apparently from a spark produced during the erection of steelwork to extend the shop onto the site of Henry Crellin's kipper shop at No. 32. The whole building was alight in next to no time and could not be saved. However, within a week Woolworths had reached agreement with the owners of the Palais de Danse on the opposite side of the street to move there temporarily. The fire-damaged site was completely cleared, and an entirely new Woolworths store erected. These two pictures show the gutted remains being cleared.

The Palais de Danse in Strand Street had a red brick frontage and originally opened as Johnson's shop. In 1927 land at the rear was cleared, and a huge ballroom constructed for the Strand Cinema Company. These two photographs, taken a short interval apart, show the building first as the Palais de Danse and then as F. W. Woolworth. These premises were opened on Friday 27th April 1951, just 16 days after the fire. In the mid-1960s they became the Maypole Supermarket and incorporated the business of Lipton's who had been two doors away. Ironically, there was also a fire in the Maypole on 13th February 1967. The building pictured was subsequently demolished along with many others in the row. A 'lookalike' red brick facade was built and the resulting building is now occupied by Waterstones, though not on exactly the same footprint.

Two interior views of the Palais de Danse in 1951, before Woolworths moved in. The first view is looking toward the Strand Street entrance while the second looks toward the stage; both show a good view of the sprung dance floor. Admission to late night dancing was advertised at 2/6 (12½ pence). When Woolworths vacated the building it was used to house several retail businesses before becoming the Maypole and then a Barry Noble amusement arcade and bingo hall.

In the years following the Second World War, Douglas Corporation embarked on a programme of building new council houses at Spring Valley and Willaston. Here are two views of work on Spring Valley estate in 1947. *Left*: Looking towards Castletown at the start of the work.

Below: Looking towards Quarterbridge, when the houses, set back behind their own access road, had reached roof level. Unlike the previous housing schemes at Hillside Avenue, Olympia and Pulrose, these properties were designed 'in-house' by Douglas Corporation.

The following two photographs, taken in 1953, are part of a series showing the possibilities of advertising on Isle of Man Road Services and Douglas Corporation Transport buses. *Left:* Lord Street bus station with Leyland Titan PD2 double deckers. The Albert Hotel, the Road Services Ltd's waiting room and enquiries desk with staff canteen, plus James Lay's outfitters, are in the background. On the right can just be seen scaffolding on the new Manx Co-operative Emporium, which was nearing completion.

Below: Victoria Street with a Corporation AEC Regent III at the terminus stop for the Upper Douglas service. Yates's Wine Lodge, the Regal Cinema and Tourist Board visitors' enquiry bureau are in the background. The photograph was taken when Victoria Street had two-way traffic.

The next sequence of photographs is part of a comprehensive series of more than a dozen views, taken in November 1948 from various viewpoints. Glen Falcon House occupied a large plot of land bounded by Broadway, Derby Road and Glen Falcon Road. Following purchase by Douglas Corporation from the Okell's Trustees the house was demolished to allow widening of Broadway and Derby Road, while the garden was reduced in size and transformed into Glen Falcon. Mr. Okell's private bowling green became a flat grass area for sun-bathing. The kitchen garden across the road became the public Rose Garden.

Glen Falcon House viewed from the bottom of Murray's Road. In addition to the house and grounds, there was also a substantial stable block at the corner of Derby Road/Glen Falcon Road. The house had been occupied by W. H. Okell, son of Dr Okell the founder of the brewery. It was W. H. Okell who called in Baillie Scott, the famous locally-based Arts and Crafts architect, to redesign the interior. Illustrations of his work appeared in the architectural press of the time. After Baillie Scott had left the Island (1901) he produced plans for the distinctive entrance porch which appears in the picture.

Looking down Broadway, the demolition of Glen Falcon House is well under way in this view. Gone from the left-hand side of the building is a large greenhouse and retail shop for Okell's ales. A number of Baillie Scott-designed items from the house were salvaged by local builder L. L. Corkill, who presented them to the Manx Museum many years later. Note the illuminated directional signs on the lamp-post to the right.

Looking up Derby Road from Broadway, with the rear boundary wall to the glen being built. In the new glen a memorial plaque to the memory of T. E. Brown was set up by the World Manx Association, and unveiled by the Lt. Governor Sir Ambrose Dundas Flux Dundas. On the left of the picture the high stone wall to the Villa Marina grounds was replaced by railings that are still in place today.

This view along Glen Falcon Road shows the stable block and coach house which form part of the Glen Falcon House estate. In the centre of the picture, in front of Stanley Terrace, was the kitchen garden which was later transformed into the Rose Garden.

The bulk of the Keig Collection, unsurprisingly, concentrates on Douglas, but there are some photographs from elsewhere on the Island and a few of these are reproduced on the following pages:

Ballig Bridge, with a steam traction engine turning left into the Poortown Road. This view illustrates the significant hump in the road, along with a pronounced kink prior to realignment. On the opposite side of the road a thatched cottage and another thatched building are to be seen. It was whilst the bridge and road were being realigned that the George Formby film 'No Limit' was made, in which a motorcyclist rode off the road, down a plank into the river, and up the other side.

A very rural view of the Peel Road, with Greeba Castle and Greeba Towers in the background. Both were built to the designs of local self-taught architect John Robinson, whose many other projects included the Falcon Cliff and Douglas Head Hotel. The most famous occupier of Greeba Castle was the Victorian novelist Hall Caine, one of the most popular writers of his time. Though not a Keig photograph as such (the origin is unknown), this image is included as it forms part of the collection and is of some historic interest.

The Tynwald ceremony may not change much, but the style of clothing certainly does. The little girl in the foreground is blissfully unaware that the photographer has captured the moment on film! The Lieutenant Governor and the Lord Bishop are just descending the steps of the hill to process between the two lines of soldiers with fixed bayonets. Note the Union flag flying above Tynwald Hill; later, when flagpoles were placed on either side of the processional way, it was once again the Union flag that was flown. The familiar Three Legs flag that is seen everywhere today was only made the official flag of the Isle of Man in 1930.

Peel Harbour, with part of the fishing fleet and St Peter's Church tower dominating the background. No doubt the crew are offering helpful advice to those doing the work. The quayside contained a mixture of warehouses, commercial buildings and private houses. Notice that each fishing boat has a small rowing boat attached to it. The two boats in the foreground are strangely at right-angles to the quayside wall, rather than parallel to it. Again, this is part of the Keig Collection rather than a Keig original photograph.

Peel Harbour and Castle. Note the absence of a road leading to the breakwater and the castle steps leading right down to the harbour bottom to provide access to the other side. The timber frames of the 1860 Abernathy breakwater are clearly seen in the background. When the Victoria Pier in Douglas was complete the large crane 'Hercules' was shipped by barge to build the solid breakwater that we see today. Again, this view may not be a Keig original image.

It is a shame that no date appears on the original negative of this photograph of Ballasalla, which shows the Whitestone Inn to the left and the Douglas Road leading off to the right. The presence of the two horse-drawn stiff carts emphasises the rural nature of the village at the time the picture was taken. Visitors arriving by train would alight at Ballasalla and walk to Rushen Abbey through the centre of the village. Later they would continue upriver to Silverdale as well. In the centre of the picture is the Ballasalla Wesleyan Methodist Chapel built in 1893. It closed in 1980 and was demolished the following year; the site is now occupied by a pair of semi-detached houses.

Castletown Harbour entrance, with St Mary's Church in the left background. The uppermost octagonal part of the tower was removed in 1912 due to rotten timbers. The photograph shows a collection of houses, stables, and slaughterhouses around the Old Grammar School. It was taken prior to the construction of the lifeboat house and slipway. Also missing from the photograph is the swing pedestrian bridge of 1903.

Port St Mary harbour with a number of topsail schooners present, many of which would have been locally-built yet sailed around the world. All Port St Mary and Port Erin boats were registered in Castletown. Above the mast of CT80 is the red-brick Carrick Bay Hotel, originally built as the Golf Links by the Douglas builder F. G. Callow, who married a Port St Mary girl.

Port Erin harbour at low-tide. At this time Port Erin was a very small fishing village, with just a group of cottages along the shoreline. The arrival of the railway and of William Milner saw it flourish as a holiday destination. Milner built the Falcon's Nest Hotel, here shown in the centre of the picture on the skyline. To the left of this is his own house 'The Rest'. Between the masts of the two fishing boats can be seen St Catherine's Church, which he built in 1879. In 1894 it was extended seaward, and a tower was added, due to the ever-increasing population of the expanding village.

Above: Early motoring on the Island, taken in Albert Street, Douglas, in 1889. The driver of the car is George Gilmour, the pioneer of the telephone service in the Isle of Man. Mr Gilmour's first wife stands at the front of the car, while his daughter holds the family dog at the rear.

Right: An April 1907 scene at Kirby, the home of the Drinkwater family just outside Douglas – the Drinkwaters were amongst the early pioneers of the motor car on the Isle of Man. The Manx Automobile Club was formed in March 1905 with George Drinkwater as President, George Brown as Secretary and George Gilmour as Treasurer. At the time it was estimated that there were some 20 motorists on the Island.

Queen's Pier, Ramsey, c1900. Opened in 1886, the pier had a berthing head running at right angles at its seaward end. Steam Packet boats travelling to and from Northern Ireland and Scotland would call here as they passed by. It was here that King Edward VII, and later George VI, landed on their brief visits to the Island. The pier is a Registered Building and whilst the kiosks and all the railings have been removed since the closure of the pier in 1991, they are still held in storage.

South Ramsey viewed from Queen's Pier. Maughold Street runs ahead into the background to the rear of the promenade. Following the construction of the pier many of the properties in the picture became boarding houses. Several had rear outlets built on to increase the number of bedrooms whilst some had an extra storey or two added. The promenade by the Mooragh was being developed at this time with brand new boarding houses and hotels, but delays in the construction of the swing bridge (built 1892) meant those nearer the pier picked up most of the trade.

An early view of Ramsey, with the area which later became the Mooragh Park, opened in 1887. The Sulby River discharged to the sea here until North Shore Road and the Mooragh Promenade enclosed the area. From the dress of the people in the picture it could well be dated in the 1870s. On the right are some of the buildings at the shipyard which provided major employment for the town. On the left are the North and South Piers, built to provide a sheltered passageway into the harbourside. At the end of the South Pier stands the Lifeboat House, built in 1869. Against the harbour wall can just be made out a Steam Packet paddle steamer. It has two funnels set close together with the first just in line with the front of the paddlebox; it could therefore be *Douglas* (II), which was in service between 1864 and 1889.